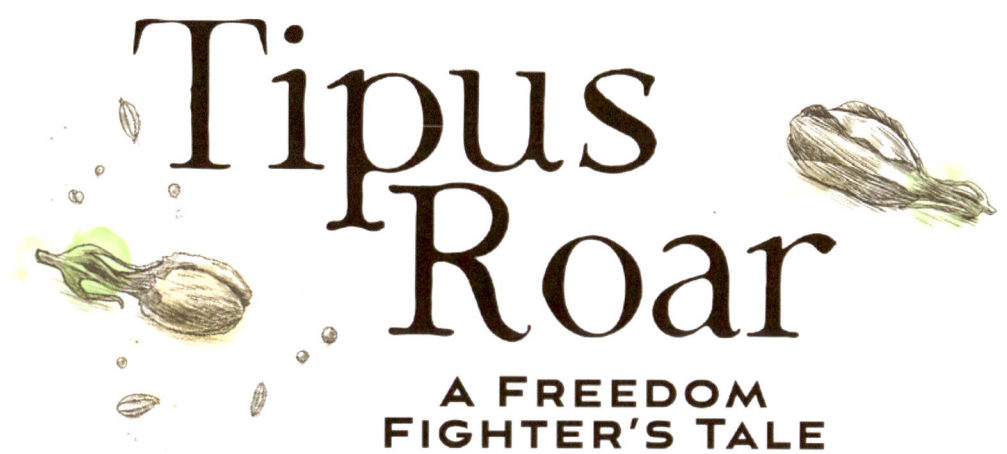

Tipus Roar
A Freedom Fighter's Tale

Written by
Subia J. Ali

Art by
Gabriel Sorondo

Copyright © 2023 Subia J. Ali

All rights reserved. Published in United States of America by Ibex Reads. No part of this book may be used or reproduced in any form without prior written permission of the author or publisher.

Written by Subia J. Ali

Illustrated by Gabriel Sorondo

Library of Congress Cataloging-in-Publication Data

Title: Tipu's Roar: A Freedom Fighter's Tale

Written by Subia J. Ali and illustrated by Gabriel Sorondo

First Edition 2023 / Riverside, California

ISBN: 9798987745427 (hardcover)

LCCN: 2023916197

[1.*Biography-Nonfiction* 2.*Colonialism* 3.*South Asian hero*]

This book was written responsibly by a human author.

Dedicated to the children of Palestine,
and the many people who have been
colonized around the world.

You are the descendants of heroes.

What is a freedom fighter?
A person who takes part in a movement against oppression and injustice.

What is colonization?
To take over a region or country by force.

What is imperialism?
To build colonies and take control of the politics and resources of a people by force.

Tipu's Roar

A Freedom Fighter's Tale

Written by
Subia J. Ali

Art by
Gabriel Sorondo

Grandpa told me he felt most gentlemanly when he wore his dress pants and bush shirt. I chuckled at him calling his button-down a bush shirt. "I forgot you don't call it that. The British made these shirts to wear in the hot climates of the countries they were exploring. Sometimes they called them safari shirts," he said as he straightened his collar.

"Bush shirt . . . like the Australian bush or the outback, Grandpa?"
"Yes, but call me Dada Jaan, not Grandpa."
"But Dada Jaan and Grandpa mean the same thing."
"Do they?" he asked softly, touching his chai-colored cheek. "Grandpa means grandest father. Dada Jaan means paternal grandfather who is my life and love. They don't mean the same thing, child."

Dada Jaan gestured with his hands, offering me a seat on the wicker chair. I sat like a princess, with my dress splayed out over my knees. My legs dangled freely beneath it. I knew a story sat on Dada Jaan's lips, waiting to be told. I was eager to hear it, just like all the times I'd listened to his intriguing tales when I was visiting from America. Dada Jaan looked out into the distance at a scrawny curry tree in his yard as if he were reading something written on its leaves.

Then he told me that the names and titles we are given are meaningful.
"They can be so important that they have the potential to change our lives forever. Sometimes if a person is proud of the name they are given, they can even change the world."

One such person with a powerful name, said Dada Jaan, was Tipu Sultan, who people called the Tiger of Mysore. Some say he earned his name as a young man by subduing a wild tiger who had attacked his friend and for never backing down from a threat.

"What do you think he was able to do with a name like that?" Dada Jaan tilted his head bird-like toward me as he spoke. Not knowing the answer, I shook my head side to side.

"Tipu Sultan became the ruler of Mysore," said Dada Jaan, explaining to me that Mysore was a kingdom in India and Tipu Sultan was a freedom fighter. He fought the British, who had come to colonize the Indian subcontinent. His unrelenting courage against the oppressors was compared to a tiger's roar.

Dada Jaan told me that the British East India Company was a powerful company used by the British Empire in the 1700's to insert their imperial rule and take over all of India, its people, and all its wealth—its tea, cotton, precious gems, and spices.

"The only person that stood in their way to the end was Tipu the Tiger, and his roar for freedom," said Dada Jaan. "He had military training and political education. He studied Islam, spoke many languages, and was a pioneer in rocket artillery so he could defend his people against the colonial forces," my grandfather explained to me.

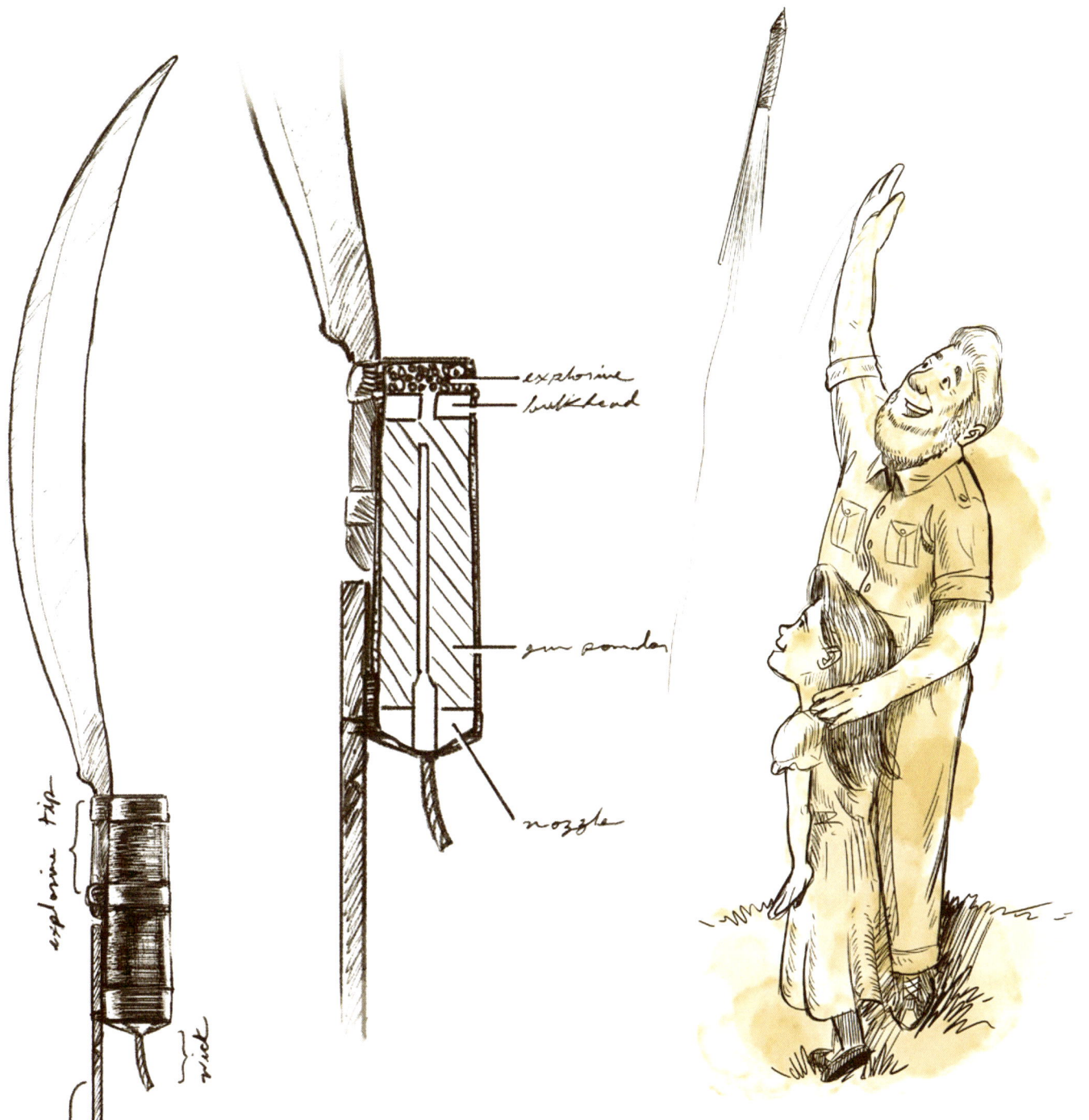

"His rockets were among his greatest innovations," Dada Jaan went on. "His scientific design made with gun powder, metal tubes, and swords revolutionized the weapon. The British suffered heavily from Tipu's rockets. They quickly adopted it, as did others around the world."

"Shooooo!" Dada Jaan shot his arm to the sky, imitating the launch of a screeching rocket. I giggled at his funny sound.

When Tipu was only 15 years old, his father, Hyder Ali, assigned him to lead 20,000 soldiers into battle. He was, of course, victorious. Tipu charmed and made peace treaties with other regions of India that had been coerced into siding with the British. With his father by his side, Tipu took many British-held cities and forts, weakening the overconfident invaders.

"Can you imagine how many others wanted to join the famous Tipu the Tiger?" Dada Jaan whispered, and I leaned in closer to find out. There were the French, who fought alongside Tipu's armies as allies, Dada Jaan told me. The Americans, too, who were fighting for their own independence from Britain, revered the brave leaders Hyder Ali and his son, Tipu.

"The great naval battle of Delaware Bay in America's revolution against Britain was won thanks to a formidable ship that was named the Hyder Ali." Americans even wrote poems and sang songs about their friends in the East, my grandfather said proudly. "It seemed the whole world was fighting for their freedom from the British and stood in solidarity with each other." I listened wide-eyed as Dada Jaan spoke.

W hen Tipu's father, Hyder Ali, died, Tipu became the Sultan of Mysore and continued to repel the British from his soil. His name and his famous tiger symbol were emblazoned on everything and struck fear in his enemies.

As America gained its independence from Britain, France was beginning a revolution of their own and could no longer help their allies in India. The British were now free to pour their troops and resources into the war on Tipu's Mysore, the last standing kingdom in India.

Eventually, the British would take all of India and Tipu would die in battle, valiantly defending his territory. His enemies would try to rewrite history and Tipu's legacy—as colonizers and dubious politicians tend to do—but India's famous freedom fighter's name and roar would echo throughout time in spite of this, said Dada Jaan.

"Oh, no." I slumped into my chair on hearing of Tipu's defeat. Dada Jaan laughed. "It's alright, child. Just remember Tipu Sultan's famous words, "To live like a lion for a day is far better than to live for a hundred years like a jackal."

I forced a small smile to hide my disappointment over the ending of his story. Dada Jaan patted my head and went into his room to change and offer his evening prayer. I sat still, watching a bird dangerously dodge the curry tree. I wondered how different things would have been if Tipu Sultan had won against the British. Would Dada Jaan still think he looked most gentlemanly in his bush shirt?

"Years later, Dada Jaan visited my parents and me in America. One evening he stood on our driveway watching the sunset and a breeze lifted the edge of his all-white traditional tunic. The full head of hair on his head and groomed beard had turned entirely white. It looked striking against his even brown skin. I quietly watched him from the garage. He stood tall, like a pillar. To me, he looked more gentlemanly now than he ever did in his bush shirt.

"To live like a lion for a day is far better
than to live for a hundred years like a jackal."

- Tipu Sultan 1751-1799

www.ingramcontent.com/pod-product-compliance
Lightning Source LLC
Chambersburg PA
CBRC091212010526
44119CB00021B/377